For Alison – with thanks for getting me started – W.C.
For Mo – S.M.

All the Colours of the Earth copyright © Frances Lincoln Limited 2004
Selection copyright © Wendy Cooling 2004
Illustrations copyright © Sheila Moxley 2004

First published in Great Britain in 2004 by
Frances Lincoln Children's Books,
4 Torriano Mews, Torriano Avenue, London NW5 2RZ
www.franceslincoln.com

British Library Cataloguing in Publication Data
available on request

ISBN 1-84507-014-3

Printed in Singapore
1 3 5 7 9 8 6 4 2

All the Colours of the Earth

Poems from Around the World

Wendy Cooling
Illustrated by Sheila Moxley

FRANCES LINCOLN CHILDREN'S BOOKS

CONTENTS

Introduction

All around the world children play, talk and sing together. The poems in this book show what children share as well as reflecting the differences in their lives and the need to protect their world.

The poets come from every corner of the earth and all have strong voices. They invite us to enjoy the magic of words and the power of language. Their voices are informed by the sounds and traditions of their own childhoods and by the international issues and concerns of today. They ask us to think about the world – its richness and its inequalities – and leave us with a sense of hope for the future.

These poems are about seeing ourselves not just as members of a street, village or city community, but as citizens of the world.

Enjoy them!

All the colours of the earth

Children come in all the colours of the earth –
The roaring browns of bears and soaring eagles,
The whispering golds of late summer grasses
And crackling russets of fallen leaves,
The tinkling pinks of tiny seashells by the rumbling sea.
Children come with hair like bouncy baby lambs,
Or hair that flows like water,
Or hair that curls like cats in snoozy cat colours.
Children come in all the colours of love,
In endless shades of you and me.
For love comes in cinnamon, walnut and wheat,
Love is amber and ivory and ginger and sweet
Like caramel, and chocolate, and the honey of bees.
Dark as leopard spots, light as sand,
Children buzz with laughter that kisses our land,
With sunlight like butterflies happy and free.
Children come in all the colours of the earth and sky and sea.

Sheila Hamanaka
USA

Supermarket

I'm
lost
among a
maze of cans
behind a pyramid
of jams, quite near
asparagus and rice,
close to the Oriental spice,
and just before sardines.
I hear my mother calling, "Joe.
Where are you, Joe?
Where did you
Go?" And I reply in a voice concealed among
the candied orange peel, and packs of Chocolate
Dreams.
"I
hear
you, Mother
dear, I'm here –
quite near the ginger ale
and beer, and lost among a
maze
of cans
behind a
pyramid of jams

GOLDEN
FLAKES
DEN

quite near asparagus
and rice, close to the
Oriental spice, and just before sardines."

But
still
my mother
calls me, "Joe!
Where are you, Joe?
Where did you go?"
"Somewhere
around asparagus
that's in a sort of
broken glass,
beside a kind of m-
ess-
y jell
that's near a tower of cans that
f
e
l
l

and squashed the Chocolate Dreams."

Felice Holman
USA

chocolate
SPECIAL
OFFER
Dreams

11

Fruits

mangoes
 and ripe bananas
 jelly coconut
 and pomegranates
jack-fruit
 and stinking-toe
june plum
and nase-berry
sweetsop
and sour-sop
tamarind
and jimbeli
cane-juice
 and coolie-plum
 star-apple
 and custard-apple
navel orange
 and wild cherries

fruits everywhere
 brimming with life
 spread out in front
 of market women
 buy some
 and experience delight

Opal Palmer Adisa
Jamaica/USA

12

Imagine

My friend Shahiz has a granny in India.
 Well, her dad's granny really.
  She lives in a village in the forest
   where there's no TV no cars or make-up kits
   and no one goes to school!
   I really like that bit
   but stared at Shiraz when she told me.
   "Can't imagine it!" I said.

 "In our village no one has to live alone,
  or in a Home," she said.
  "At night people tell each other stories
  about the village long ago,
 or from the Mahabharata
  – they all remember different parts
 and sit in darkness, under stars,
sharing in the telling.
 Far away a panther coughs, monkeys screech,
but everyone listens to Krishna's adventures."
"Can't imagine it," I said...
It's different, innit, when it's not on telly,
 when your best mate tells you
 and that's someone like Shahiz –
  dead cool, purple highlights in her hair...

 I stared at her,
  tried to imagine living in that village,
   tried to see myself there... but couldn't.

Joan Poulson
UK

Surrounded by noise

Surrounded by Noise!
I'm surrounded by noise,
LISTEN!
BEEP! BEEP! BEEP!
A car down on the street.
BOOGIE! BOOGIE! BOOGIE!
A disco beat.
THUMP! THUMP! THUMP!
A hammer next door.
THUD! THUD! THUD!
Brother jumping on the floor.
CLACKETY! CLACKETY! CLACKETY!
A train rattles by.
ROAR! ROAR! ROAR!
A plane climbs the sky.
DRILL! DRILL DRILL!
A workman on the road.
NO! NO! NO!
Mum about to explode.
We're surrounded by noise,
Just. STOP!
Just. LISTEN!

Ian Souter
UK

It is impossible

It is impossible
for anyone to enter
our small world.
The adults don't
understand us
they think
we're childish.
No one can get in
our world.
It has a wall twenty feet high
and adults
have only ten feet ladders.

Ross Falconer
Australia

16

I am

I am a human being, a boy.
You may say I am a special compound which can
Think, can see... etc,
And a little bit different from cat, dog, etc.
You may say I am a body with a soul
which is living.
I have a special computer which requires no electricity.
It is in my skull.
It works all the time until night.
When it can't work, I can't work.
I have a special pump which pumps the blood all over
my body, and no electricity required.
It is in my left chest,
But it never stops or feels tired.
When it stops, I stop.
I have some other machines which require no electricity
And they never stop or feel tired.
But when they stop, I stop.
That's me.

However, I am still I!

Chun Po Man
Hong Kong

One for a tangle

One for a tangle,
One for a curl,
One for a boy,
One for a girl,
One to make a parting,
One to tie a bow,
One to blow the cobwebs out
And one to make it grow.

Traditional

Granny Granny please comb my hair

Granny Granny please comb my hair
you always take your time
you always take such care

You put me on a cushion between your knees
you rub a little coconut oil
parting gentle as a breeze

Mummy Mummy
she's always in a hurry-hurry
rush
she pulls my hair
sometimes she tugs

But Granny
you have all the time
in the world and when you're finished
you always turn my head and say
"Now who's a nice girl?"

Grace Nichols
Guyana/UK

19

Skipping rope song

Salt, vinegar, mustard, pepper,
If I dare,
I can do better,
who says no?
'cause hens don't crow!
Salt, vinegar, mustard, pepper.

Salt, vinegar, mustard, pepper.
I wanna be great,
a hotshot lawyer,
a famous dancer,
a tough operator,
Salt, vinegar, mustard, pepper.

Salt, vinegar, mustard, pepper,
   If I dare
    I can do better,
     who cares from zero,
     that hens don't crow,
    Salt, vinegar, mustard, pepper.

Dionne Brand
Trinidad/Canada

Where go the boats

Dark brown is the river,
Golden is the sand.
It flows along for ever,
With trees on either hand.

Green leaves a-floating,
Castles of the foam,
Boats of mine a-boating –
Where will all come home?

On goes the river
And out past the mill,
Away down the valley,
Away down the hill.

Away down the river,
A hundred miles or more,
Other little children
Shall bring my boats ashore.

Robert Louis Stevenson
UK

Paper boats

Day by day I float my paper boats one by one
down the running stream.
In big black letters I write my name on them and
the name of the village where I live.
I hope that someone in some strange land will find them
and know who I am.
I load my little boats with shiuli flowers from our garden,
and hope that these blooms of the dawn
will be carried safely to land in the night.
I launch my paper boats and look into the sky and see
the little clouds setting their white bulging sails.
I know not what playmate of mine in the sky
sends them down the air to race with my boats!
When night comes I bury my face in my arms
and dream that my paper boats float on and on
under the mighty stars.
The fairies of sleep are sailing in them, and the
lading is their baskets full of dreams.

Rabindranath Tagore
India

The swing

How do you like to go up in a swing,
Up in the air so blue?
Oh, I do think it the pleasantest thing
Ever a child can do!

Up in the air and over the wall,
Till I can see so wide,
Rivers and trees and cattle and all
Over the countryside –

Till I look down on the garden green,
Down on the roof so brown –
Up in the air I go flying again,
Up in the air and down!

Robert Louis Stevenson
UK

Swinging

Push me, Mummy, push me
High up in the air,
Higher, Mummy, higher,
Send me over there

Where that branch is growing,
This is so much fun!
Let me touch those leaves, Mummy,
Let me touch the sun.

Swing me, Mummy, swing me,
Do you call this high?
Let me touch that house there, Mummy,
Let me touch the sky.

Stop me, Mummy, stop me,
Get me off this swing!
My ears are popping, Mummy,
My head is starting to ring.

Oh the ground is spinning!
I think I'm going to die.
Really, Mummy, why did you
Push the swing so high?

Valerie Bloom
Jamaica/UK

Kite

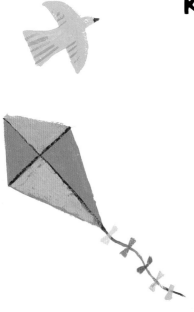

A kite on the ground
    is just paper and string
      but up in the air
        it will dance and sing.
      A kite in the air
        will dance and will caper
          but back on the ground
            is just string and paper.

Anonymous

Lament on losing a kite

Aue! Aue!
My kite string's bust!
My kite's gone off,
It's lost in space,
It's gone for good!

All right, kite:
Fly on a visit.
Visit here and visit there –
Old Wind has got you now.

And where have you gone –
To the home of the stars?
Where are you clinging –
To the breast of the sky?

Aue! My kite's flown off,
It's tangled with the far side of the sky.
Its head is hanging down
All drooping in the wind.

That string snapped in my hands,
Snapped under my foot –

Useless end of string!
Now I'm starting to cry –
I sound like a startled duck.
        It is *lost!*

Maori chant
Native New Zealand

There is joy

There is joy in
Feeling the warmth
Come to the great world
And seeing the sun
Follow its old footprints
In the summer night.

There is fear in
Feeling the cold
Come to the great world
And seeing the moon
– Now new moon, now full moon –
Follow its old footprints
In the winter night.

Anonymous
Inuit

Four seasons

Spring is showery, flowery, bowery.
Summer: hoppy, choppy, poppy.
Autumn: wheezy, sneezy, freezy.
Winter: slippy, drippy, nippy.

Anonymous
UK

Winter trees

Aren't you cold and won't you freeze,
With branches bare, you winter trees?
You've thrown away your summer shift,
Your autumn gold has come adrift.

Dearie me, you winter trees,
What strange behaviour if you please!
In summer, you could wear much less,
But come the winter, you undress!

Zoltán Zelk
translated by George Szirtes
Hungary

I am a tree

I am a tree.

Like you
I breathe,
I reproduce.
I too need the warmth of the sun,
The wetness of the rain,
The space to grow.
One difference between us two
Is that
You need me
More than I need you.

Pat Moon
UK

The pines

Hear the rumble,
Oh, hear the crash.
The great trees tumble.
The strong boughs smash.

Men with saws
Are cutting the pines –
That marched like soldiers
In straight green lines.

Seventy years
Have made them tall.
It takes ten minutes
To make them fall.

And breaking free
With never a care,
The pine cones leap
Through the clear, bright air.

Margaret Mahy
New Zealand

Hurt no living thing

Hurt no living thing,
Ladybird nor butterfly,
Nor moth with dusty wing,
Nor cricket chirping cheerily,
Nor grasshopper, so light of leap,
Nor dancing gnat,
Nor beetle fat,
Nor harmless worms that creep.

Christina Rossetti
UK

Can you?

Can you sell me the air as it slips through your fingers
As it slaps at your face and untidies your hair?
Perhaps you could sell me fivepennyworth of wind
or more, perhaps sell me a storm?
Perhaps the elegant air
you would sell me, that air
(not all of it) which trips around
your garden, from corolla to corolla
in your garden for the birds
tenpence worth of elegant air?
      The air spins and goes by
      in a butterfly.
      Belongs to no one, no one.

Can you sell me the sky
the sky sometimes blue
or grey as well sometimes
a strip of your sky
the bit you think you bought with the trees
of your garden, as one buys the roof with the house?
Can you sell me a dollar
of sky, two miles
of sky, a slice, whatever you can
of your sky?

> The sky is in the clouds
> The clouds go by
> Belong to no one, no one.

Nicolás Guillén
Cuba

The people in poverty

I came to a place
where they dump
all the garbage of the town.

And I saw some children
filling a few old sacks
with rusty tins
worn-out shoes
bits of old cardboard boxes.

and some flies crept in among the sacks
and then came out
and settled on the children's heads.

Gloria Guevara
translated by Peter Wright
Nicaragua

It makes me furious!

When I come upon a child
sad, dirty, skinny
it makes me furious!

When I see food
tossed into the garbage
and a poor man poking around in case
it isn't rotten yet
it makes me furious!

When a toothless woman
hunched and old tells me
she's 26
it makes me furious!

When a little old man sleeps
by his final corner
it makes me furious!

When the poor wait
for the rich man to finish his business
to ask him
for last week's salary
it makes me furious!

Teresa de Jesús
Chile

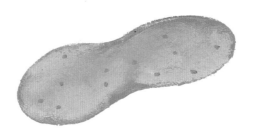

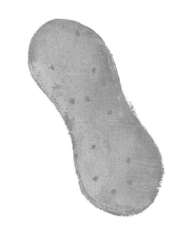

Mix a pancake

Mix a pancake,
Stir a pancake,
Pop it in the pan;
Fry the pancake,
Toss the pancake –
Catch it if you can!

Christina Rossetti
UK

I had a nickel

I had a nickel and I walked around the block.
I walked right into a baker's shop.
I took two doughnuts right out of the grease;
I handed the lady my five-cent piece.
She looked at the nickel and she looked at me,
And said, 'This money's no good to me
There's a hole in the nickel, and it goes right through.'
Says I, 'There's a hole in the doughnut, too.'

Anonymous
USA

Traditional Chinese saying

When eating bamboo sprouts,
Remember the man
who planted them.

All we need

Food in our bellies
Hats on our heads
Water to quench us
Sheets on our beds.

Teachers to teach us
Shoes on our feet
Trousers and T-shirts
Shelter and heat.

Someone to love us
Someone to love
Hope for the future
Light from above.

Steve Turner
UK

I'd like to squeeze

I'd like to squeeze this round world
into a new shape

I'd like to squeeze this round world
like a tube of toothpaste

I'd like to squeeze this round world
fair and square

I'd like to squeeze it and squeeze it
till everybody had an equal share

John Agard
Guyana/UK

41

Good hope

I believe
  There is enough food
    On this planet
      For everyone.

        I believe
          That it is possible
            For all people
              To live in peace.

          I believe
            We can live
              Without guns,
            I believe everyone
          Is important.

  I believe there are good Christians
  And good Muslims,
  Good Jews
  And good not sures,
  I believe
    There is good in everyone
      I believe in people.

    If I did not believe
      I would stop writing.

I know
  Every day
    Children cry for water,
    And every day
    Racists attack,
    Still every day
    Children play
    With no care for colour.

    So I believe **there is hope**
    And I hope
   That there are many believers
  Believing
 There is hope,
That is what I hope
And this is what I believe,
I believe in you.
Believe me.

Benjamin Zephaniah
UK

About the Poets

Opal Palmer Adisa grew up on sugar plantation in Jamaica and remembers making up stories in her head. She now lives in the USA, where she writes essays, poetry and children's stories.

John Agard grew up in Guyana. As a child he loved making up cricket commentaries. He now lives in the UK and is hugely popular as a poet and performer.

Valerie Bloom grew up in a small Jamaican village and now lives in the UK. She travels widely performing her work as a writer for adults and children.

Dionne Brand was born in Trinidad and now lives in Canada. Her poetry resonates with the rhythms of the Caribbean.

Gloria Guevara is a Nicaraguan poet. Her work is often concerned with today's social issues.

Nicholás Guillén is a contemporary poet from Cuba.

Sheila Hamanaka is an American author and illustrator. Her poem "All the colours of the Earth" was first published as a picture-book.

Felice Holman is a widely-published and respected poet who was born in the USA in 1919.

Teresa de Jesús is the pseudonym of a South American poet who wishes to remain anonymous.

Margaret Mahy has twice won the prestigious Carnegie Prize for her novels, and also writes picture-books texts, short stories and poems. She lives in New Zealand.

Chun Po Man submitted his poem "I am" to a London schools poetry competition in 1981, when he was 16.

Pat Moon gave up teaching in 1991 to be a full-time writer. She has published collections of poetry and novels for children of all ages. She lives in England.

Grace Nichols spent her early years in Guayana, in a home filled with storytelling; she moved to Georgetown when she was eight. She now lives in the UK, where she writes for adults and children.

Joan Poulson writes for children and grown-ups, and frequently gives readings at literary festivals.

Christina Rossetti (1830-94) is one of England's best-loved poets.

Robert Louis Stevenson was born in Edinburgh in 1850 and died in Samoa in 1894. He is best remembered for his novel *Treasure Island* and his collection of poetry *A Child's Garden of Verses*.

Rabrindranath Tagore (1861-1941) is one of India's most famous poets.

Steve Turner is a poet and biographer living in the United Kingdom. His own children inspired him to start writing children's poetry. Steve visits schools and bookshops reading his work.

Zoltán Zelk (1906-81) is a Hungarian children's poet and writer who spent half his life working as a labourer. He was imprisoned for a time during the 1950s following the Hungarian Revolution.

Benjamin Zephaniah is a celebrated performance poet with a finger firmly on the pulse of today's Britain. As well as poetry collections, he has recently published two acclaimed novels for children.

Acknowledgements

The publishers would like to thank the following for permission to include in-copyright material: Walker Books for "Fruits" by Opal Palmer Adisa from *A Caribbean Dozen* ed. by John Agard and Grace Nichols; the Caroline Sheldon Literary Agency for "I'd Like To Squeeze" by John Agard from *Get Back Pimple* (Viking); John Johnson for "Lament on Losing A Kite" by Anthony Alpers from *Legends of the South Seas* (John Murray); Eddison Pearson for "Swinging" by Valerie Bloom from *Let Me Touch the Sky* (Macmillan); Harper Collins for "All the Colors of the Earth" from *All the Colors of the Earth* copyright (c) 1994 Sheila Hamanaka; Orion Children's Books for "The Pines" by Margaret Mahy; Curtis Brown Ltd, London for "Granny Granny Please Comb My Hair" by Grace Nichols; Hodder Children's Books for "Imagine" by Joan Poulson from *Pictures in My Mind* (Macdonald Young Books); Lion Publishing for "All We Need" by Steve Turner from *The Day I Fell Down the Toilet*; George Szirtes for his translation of "Winter Trees" by Zoltán Zelk from *Sheep Don't Go to School* (Bloodaxe); Viking for "Good Hope" by Benjamin Zephaniah from *Funky Chickens*.

The publishers apologise to any copyright holders they were unable to trace and would like to hear from them.